HAL•LEONARD®
VIOLIN PLAY-ALONG

VOL. 40

AUDIO ACCESS INCLUDED

PLAYBACK+
Speed · Pitch · Balance · Loop

Trans-Siberian Orchestra

T0055807

RECORDINGS!

To access audio visit:
www.halleonard.com/mylibrary

Enter Code
2375-8715-7370-1719

7777 W. BLUEMOUND RD. P.O BOX 13819 MILWAUKEE, WI 53213

ISBN: 978-1-4803-4554-6

In Australia Contact:
Hal Leonard Australia Pty. Ltd.
4 Lentara Court
Cheltenham, Victoria, 3192 Australia
Email: ausadmin@halleonard.com.au

Visit Hal Leonard Online at
www.halleonard.com

CONTENTS

Page   Title

4   Christmas Eve/Sarajevo 12/24

6   Dreams of Fireflies

8   First Snow

10   A Mad Russian's Christmas

14   The Mountain

16   Mozart and Memories

20   Siberian Sleigh Ride

22   Wizards in Winter

Christmas Eve/Sarajevo 12/24

Music by Paul O'Neill and Robert Kinkel

Dreams of Fireflies

Music by Paul O'Neill

First Snow

Music by Paul O'Neill

9

A Mad Russian's Christmas

Music by Paul O'Neill, Robert Kinkel and Peter Ilyich Tchaikovsky

molto rit.

Allegro

The Mountain

By Edvard Grieg, Paul O'Neill and Jon Oliva

Mozart and Memories

Music by Paul O'Neill and Jon Oliva
(Based upon SYMPHONY NO. 25 by Wolfgang Amadeus Mozart)

Siberian Sleigh Ride

Music by Paul O'Neill

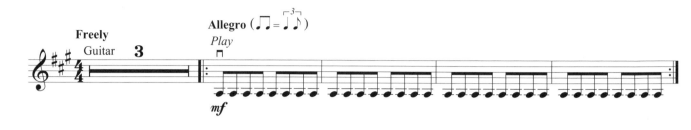

Wizards in Winter

Music by Paul O'Neill and Robert Kinkel